Catherine Quévremont

Lasagne

Photographs by Hiroko Mori
Styling by Sandra Mahut

contents

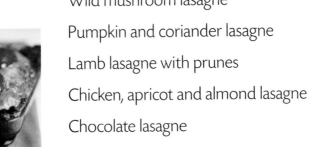

tricks of the trade

Tomato sauce

Makes 500 ml (18 fl oz) of sauce
1 kg (2¼ lb) large, ripe tomatoes
2 garlic cloves
1 onion
3 tablespoons olive oil
1 teaspoon sugar
1 sprig fresh rosemary
1 sprig fresh thyme
½ bunch fresh basil
salt and freshly ground black pepper

Plunge the tomatoes into boiling water for 1 minute. Pierce with the point of a sharp knife and remove the skins. Cut in half, discard the seeds and roughly chop the flesh. Peel and finely chop the garlic and onion. Heat the oil in a frying pan and lightly fry the garlic, onion and tomatoes. Add the sugar, thyme and rosemary, and season with salt and three turns of the peppermill. Simmer, uncovered, over low heat for 30 minutes. Rinse the basil and blot dry with kitchen paper. When the sauce is cooked, pour into a food processor or electric blender, add the basil leaves and process to a fine consistency. This sauce will keep in the refrigerator for 2-3 days - simply pour into a screw-top jar, drizzle with olive oil and close.

Béchamel sauce

Makes 500 ml (18 fl oz) of sauce
75 g (3 oz) butter
1 heaped tablespoon plain flour
500 ml (18 fl oz) milk
nutmeg
salt and freshly ground pepper

Melt the butter in a heavy-bottomed pan. Remove from the heat and add the flour, stirring briskly so that it is absorbed by the butter and forms a smooth paste. Add a little of the milk and stir well in - there is no need to put the pan back on the heat as it will be hot enough to start cooking the Béchamel sauce. Continue adding a little more milk, gradually blending it with the flour and butter, until you begin to obtain a smooth, even consistency. Then return the pan to very low heat and gradually add the rest of the milk, stirring continuously until the sauce thickens. Stir gently for a further 2-3 minutes, to cook the flour. Season with salt and pepper and a little freshly grated nutmeg.

Flavouring the pasta

You can vary the taste of the pasta by flavouring the pan of boiling, salted cooking water (use 2 teaspoons coarse salt for a large pan of water) with 2 tablespoons olive oil added to prevent the lasagne sheets sticking together while they are cooking.

For a lemon flavour, add the juice of 2-3 lemons (or the equivalent of bottled lemon juice) to the cooking water for lasagnes made with fish or grilled vegetables.

For an orange flavour that goes well with shellfish or chicken, add the juice of 2 oranges to the cooking water.

For oriental-style, sweet-and-sour lasagnes made with lamb, flavour the cooking water with 1 tablespoon orange-flower water.

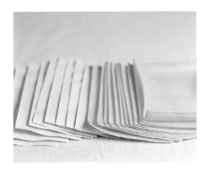

Dried or fresh pasta

A wide range of dried and fresh lasagne is available in shops and supermarkets. Fresh lasagne is more pliable and tastes more like homemade pasta. Cooking times are indicated on the packaging. The simplest option is to use lasagne that needs no precooking – use straight from the packet and simply alternate layers of pasta with the sauce. For best results with this type of pasta, the sauce should be quite liquid – the lasagne sheets absorb the extra liquid and are much softer.

Lasagne sheets that need precooking take a little more time and effort but the result is deliciously smooth. Cook the sheets according to manufacturer's instructions and then rinse under the cold tap or in a basin of cold water to stop them cooking. Drain and blot dry with kitchen paper and then alternate layers of pasta with the lasagne sauce.

Homemade lasagne is more pliable and often thicker and therefore needs to be cooked for a little longer.

Pasta sheets vary in size and thickness. Although we have allowed 8 sheets for most of our recipes, you can vary this according to the size of your lasagne and the appetite of your guests.

Homemade lasagne pasta

Makes enough for 6 people
300 g (10 oz) plain flour, or, preferably, Italian pasta flour (follow manufacturer's instructions)
3 eggs
water

Sift the flour into a pile on a work surface, make a well in the centre and crack the eggs into the well. Using the tips of your fingers (the dough is sticky at first), slowly draw the flour from the outside into the centre, mixing with the eggs to form a ball. If the dough is too dry, dampen your palms or sprinkle with a little water. Knead until smooth and elastic – divide the dough in two if difficult to work. Cover the bowl with a clean tea towel or clingfilm, and leave to stand at room temperature for 1 hour.

Lightly flour the work surface, roll out the dough until paper thin and cut to the required size (about 7.5 x 13 cm/3 x 5 inches). Alternatively, use a machine for cutting pasta – these are widely available.

The pasta can be coloured or flavoured with a variety of ingredients – well-drained, finely chopped tomatoes (red), cooked spinach, finely chopped and squeezed very dry (green), squid ink (black) or grated lemon rind.

Choosing the best cheeses

You can flavour the Béchamel sauce with:
• dry, grated goat's cheese
• grated Parmesan
• blue-veined cheese (Roquefort, Dolcelatte, Gorgonzola)
• Ricotta

You can also place thin slices of cheese between the pasta sheets. Try:
• Fontina
• Mimolette or Bel Paese
• Mozzarella

For a gratin topping, sprinkle with:
• grated Parmesan
• grated Gruyère

When the lasagne is cooked, top with:
• Parmesan shavings
• Gruyère shavings

Tomato mozzarella lasagne

Serves 4-6

8 sheets of fresh or precooked lasagne

1 kg (2¼ lb) firm tomatoes

500 g (1 lb) (about 4 balls) mozzarella

3 tablespoons olive oil

1 x 200 g (7 oz) jar pesto

100 g (3½ oz) black olives

1 bunch basil

salt and freshly ground black pepper

Preheat the oven to 180°C (350°F), gas mark 4.

Plunge the tomatoes into a saucepan of boiling water for 1 minute. Prick with the point of a sharp knife and remove the skin. Cut in half, deseed and slice the flesh. Drain the mozzarella if necessary and pat dry with kitchen paper. Cut into thin slices.

Pour some olive oil into the bottom of a baking dish and cover with a layer of lasagne sheets. Add a layer of tomato slices seasoned with salt and pepper, followed by a layer of sliced mozzarella. Spread pesto on top, to taste, then sprinkle with a few olives and some chopped basil leaves. Top with more lasagne sheets and drizzle with oil. Repeat the layers, finishing with a layer of mozzarella. Season with salt and pepper.

Bake in the preheated oven for 30-35 minutes.

Allow the lasagne to rest for 5 minutes and garnish with fresh basil leaves before serving.

Pesto lasagne

Serves 4-6

8 sheets lasagne, plain or verde (spinach), fresh or precooked if preferred

4 garlic cloves

25 basil leaves

100 g (3½ oz) pine nuts

100 g (3½ oz) grated Parmesan cheese

150 ml (5 fl oz) olive oil

salt and freshly ground black pepper

1 x 150 g (5 oz) Parmesan cheese in a piece, to serve

Preheat the oven to 180°C (350°F), gas mark 4.

Peel the garlic and remove any green shoots. Wash and dry the basil leaves. In a dry nonstick frying pan, toast the pine nuts quickly over high heat.

For the pesto, put the garlic, basil leaves, toasted pine nuts and grated Parmesan in the bowl of a food processor or blender. Begin to mix, gradually pouring in the olive oil until you obtain a thick paste. Season with salt and pepper.

If not using precooked lasagne sheets, bring a large pan of salted water to the boil, add 2 tablespoons of olive oil and cook the lasagne for the length of time recommended on the packet. Refresh in cold water, then drain on kitchen paper.

Lightly oil a baking dish and cover the bottom with a layer of lasagne. Spread with pesto, then top with another layer of lasagne. Continue layering, finishing with a layer of pesto.

Bake in the preheated oven for 25 minutes.

Remove from the oven and leave to rest for 5 minutes. Cut shavings from the piece of Parmesan cheese with a vegetable peeler and arrange on top of the lasagne before serving.

Cheese lasagne

Serves 4-6

8 sheets lasagne

200 g (7 oz) Gorgonzola cheese

250 g (9 oz) mascarpone cheese

100 g (3½ oz) grated Parmesan cheese

50 g (2 oz) finely ground walnuts

single cream (optional)

olive oil

freshly ground black pepper

Preheat the oven to 180°C (350°F), gas mark 4.

Remove the rind from the Gorgonzola and cut into small pieces. Put the mascarpone, Gorgonzola and all but 2 tablespoons of the grated Parmesan into a saucepan. Warm over low heat, stirring with a wooden spoon. The mixture should be smooth, except for a few small lumps of blue from the Gorgonzola. Stir in the ground walnuts. If the mixture is too dry, stir in some cream. Season with 3 turns of the peppermill.

If not using precooked lasagne sheets, bring a large pan of salted water to the boil, add 2 tablespoons of olive oil and cook the lasagne for the length of time recommended on the packet. Refresh in cold water, then drain on kitchen paper.

Lightly oil a baking dish. Cover the bottom of the dish with a layer of lasagne sheets and spoon over some of the cheese mixture. Continue layering until the dish is filled, topping with a layer of grated Parmesan.

Bake in the preheated oven for 25-30 minutes.

Courgette and goat's cheese lasagne

Serves 4-6

8 sheets precooked lasagne

3 medium courgettes

3 goat's cheeses

2 eggs

3½ tablespoons whipping cream

1 teaspoon ground cumin

1 tablespoon milk (optional)

olive oil

salt and freshly ground black pepper

Preheat the oven to 180°C (350°F), gas mark 4.

Wash and dry the courgettes, slice into rounds and cook for 5 minutes in boiling, salted water. Drain immediately. Using a fork, crush 2 of the goat's cheeses.

In a bowl, whisk together the eggs and cream. Add the crushed cheese and cumin. Season to taste with salt and pepper. Stir until thoroughly combined, adding a little milk to thin it out if necessary.

Lightly oil a baking dish. Pour a little of the cheese mixture in the bottom of the dish, top with some lasagne sheets and a layer of sliced courgettes. Continue layering until all the ingredients are used up.

To finish, slice the remaining goat's cheese into rounds and arrange on top of the lasagne; these will brown as it bakes.

Bake in the preheated oven for 20 minutes.

Beef and tomato lasagne

Serves 4-6

8 sheets precooked lasagne

6 hamburger patties

1 bunch basil

200 g (7 oz) sun-dried tomatoes in oil

2 x 400 g (14 oz) cans chopped tomatoes

1 teaspoon dried oregano

olive oil

100 g (3½ oz) pitted black olives, cut in half if large

salt and freshly ground black pepper

Preheat the oven to 180°C (350°F), gas mark 4.

Place the hamburger patties on a work surface and press down or pound until they are very thin. Wash and dry the basil leaves. Drain and slice the sun-dried tomatoes.

Put the canned tomatoes in a bowl. If there are any very large chunks, cut into smaller pieces. Season with salt, pepper and oregano to taste.

Lightly oil the bottom of a baking dish. Pour in some of the canned tomatoes and sprinkle with a few basil leaves. Top with 2 sheets of lasagne, 2 hamburger patties, some sun-dried tomato slices, olives, and more chopped tomato. Continue layering, finishing with a layer of chopped tomato. Season well and sprinkle with a little more oregano.

Bake in the preheated oven for 30 minutes.

Meatball lasagne

Serves 4-6

8 sheets precooked
lasagne

350 g (11 oz) ham

1/2 bunch fresh parsley

2 garlic cloves

1 onion

350 g (11 oz) minced beef

1 tablespoon dried oregano

1 egg

75 g (3 oz) butter

1 heaped tablespoon
plain flour

500 ml (18 fl oz) milk

nutmeg

4 tablespoons grated
Parmesan cheese

2 x 400 g (14 oz) cans
chopped tomatoes

5 sprigs fresh sage

100 ml (3 1/2 fl oz) olive oil

salt and freshly ground
black pepper

Place the ham in a food processor and chop finely. Wash and dry the parsley and chop finely. Peel the garlic and onion and chop finely.

In a large bowl, mix together the minced beef, ham, parsley, garlic, onion and oregano and the egg. Season with salt and pepper and mix well until thoroughly combined. Let stand for 10 minutes.

Using the butter, flour and milk, make a Béchamel sauce as described on page 4. Season with salt and pepper and add a pinch of freshly grated nutmeg and the Parmesan. Stir in the tomatoes and sage leaves; the sauce should not be too thick.

Preheat the oven to 180°C (350°F), gas mark 4.

Form the minced beef mixture into meatballs by rolling in your hands. Coat the meatballs lightly with flour. Heat a little oil in a frying pan and cook the meatballs until golden. Make sure they do not stick to one another in the pan. Transfer to kitchen paper to drain.

Lightly oil a baking dish and pour in some of the Béchamel sauce. Arrange a few lasagne sheets on top, then more sauce, then the meatballs. Continue layering until the dish is filled, finishing with a layer of the sauce.

Bake in the preheated oven for 40 minutes.

Minced beef and sausage lasagne

Serves 4-6

8 sheets lasagne

2 garlic cloves

1 onion

400 g (14 oz) sausagemeat

350 g (11 oz) minced beef

1 bunch chives

½ bunch coriander

75 g (3oz) butter

1 heaped tablespoon flour

500 ml (18 fl oz) milk

ground allspice

1 x 500 g (16 oz) carton passatta

30 g (1 oz) grated Parmesan cheese

olive oil

grated Gruyère cheese

salt and freshly ground black pepper

If not using precooked lasagne sheets, bring a large pan of salted water to the boil, add 2 tablespoons of olive oil and cook the lasagne for the length of time recommended on the packet. Refresh in cold water, then drain on kitchen paper.

Peel the garlic and onion and chop finely.

Preheat the oven to 180°C (350°F), gas mark 4.

In a nonstick pan, cook the garlic and onion until soft. Add the sausagemeat, minced beef, and the chives and coriander snipped with scissors. Cook until browned. Transfer to a food processor and mix well.

Using the butter, flour and milk, make a Béchamel sauce as described on page 4. Cook to thicken for about 10 minutes. Season with salt, pepper and a pinch of allspice. Stir in the passatta and the Parmesan cheese. Mix well.

Lightly oil a baking dish. Arrange a few sheets of lasagne on the bottom of the dish, then top with some Béchamel sauce, meat mixture, more Béchamel and another layer of lasagne. Continue layering until all the ingredients are used, finishing with a layer of lasagne.

Sprinkle with grated Gruyère cheese and bake in the preheated oven for 30-40 minutes.

Stroganoff lasagne

Serves 4-6

8 sheets precooked
lasagne

1 large onion

250 g (8 oz) button
mushrooms

2 tablespoons olive oil

2 tablespoons tomato
purée

50 g (2 oz) butter

625 g (1¼ lb) tender beef
steak, such as sirloin or
fillet, very thinly sliced

250 g (8 fl oz) crème fraîche

salt and freshly ground
black pepper

Preheat the oven to 180°C (350°F), gas mark 4.

Peel and finely chop the onion. Wipe the mushrooms and slice thinly. Heat the oil in a pan, add the onions and cook until soft. Add the mushrooms and tomato purée. Simmer gently for 10 minutes.

To prepare the stroganoff meat, melt the butter in a large pan and add the meat slices. Cook quickly over high heat to sear. Add the meat to the mushroom mixture, then add the crème fraîche and season with salt and pepper. Simmer gently for 5 minutes.

Lightly oil a baking dish. Pour some of the meat and mushroom sauce into the bottom of the dish, then top with a few sheets of lasagne. Spread an even layer of sauce on top, then cover with more sheets of lasagne. Continue layering until the dish is filled, ending with a layer of sauce.

Bake in the preheated oven for 20-25 minutes.

Aubergine and lamb lasagne

Serves 4-6

8 sheets precooked lasagne

2 large aubergines

2 tablespoons olive oil

2 garlic cloves

2 onions

400 g (14 oz) cooked lamb, cut into pieces

1 teaspoon ground cumin

1 x 200 g (7 oz) can chopped tomatoes

½ bunch coriander, leaves removed

500 ml (18 fl oz) Béchamel sauce (see recipe page 4)

salt and freshly ground black pepper

Preheat the oven to 180°C (350°F), gas mark 4.

Wash the aubergines and cut in half lengthways. Coat generously with olive oil, place in a roasting tin and bake in the preheated oven for about 15 minutes.

Peel the garlic and onion. Place in the bowl of a food processor along with the pieces of cooked lamb and the cumin. Process until finely chopped.

When the aubergines are cooked, scoop out the flesh and crush with a fork. In a pan, combine the aubergine flesh, tomatoes and 1 tablespoon of olive oil. Add the coriander leaves. Simmer until the mixture thickens. Season with salt and pepper to taste.

Lightly oil a baking dish. Pour some of the Béchamel sauce into the bottom of the dish, then build up alternate layers of lasagne sheets, lamb and onion mixture, Béchamel sauce, and the aubergine and tomato sauce.

Bake in the preheated oven for 30-35 minutes.

Chorizo lasagne

Serves 4-6

8 sheets lasagne

4 large tomatoes

4 green peppers

2 large onions

2 garlic cloves

5 tablespoons olive oil

100 ml (3½ fl oz) dry white wine, preferably Spanish

250 g (8 oz) chorizo

saffron

salt and freshly ground black pepper

Plunge the tomatoes into a saucepan of boiling water for 1 minute. Prick with the point of a sharp knife and remove the skin. Cut in half, deseed and slice the flesh thinly. Wash the peppers, remove the seeds and membranes and cut into thin strips. Peel the onions and slice thinly. Peel and crush the garlic.

If not using precooked lasagne sheets, bring a large pan of salted water to the boil, add 2 tablespoons of olive oil and cook the lasagne for the length of time recommended on the packet. Refresh in cold water, then drain on kitchen paper.

Preheat the oven to 180°C (350°F), gas mark 4.

Heat the olive oil in a large pan. Add the sliced vegetables and cook over high heat for 5 minutes, stirring frequently with a wooden spoon. Add the wine and season with salt, pepper and a pinch of saffron. Remove from the heat.

Peel the chorizo and slice into thin rounds.

Lightly oil a baking dish. Spread a layer of the vegetables over the bottom of the dish, then top with some lasagne sheets. Add another layer of vegetables, then some slices of chorizo and a layer of lasagne sheets. Continue layering, finishing with a layer of chorizo.

Bake in the preheated oven for 25-30 minutes.

Herb-stuffed lasagne

Serves 4-6

8 sheets precooked
lasagne

350 g (10 oz) cold roast
pork, or ham

1 onion

2 garlic cloves

1 kg (2¼ lb) Swiss chard

olive oil

175 ml (6 fl oz) dry white
wine

1 bunch chives

1 bunch chervil, or parsley

½ bunch coriander

2 x 400 g (14 oz) cans
chopped tomatoes

1 celery stick, finely
chopped

50 g (2 oz) grated
Parmesan cheese

salt and freshly ground
black pepper

Finely grind the meat in a food processor. Peel the onion and garlic and chop finely. Remove the green part from the Swiss chard; the white stalks are not used for this recipe. Wash the Swiss chard greens, then blanch in a large pan of boiling, salted water. Drain thoroughly in a colander, pushing down firmly with the back of a wooden spoon to squeeze out the excess moisture, then chop coarsely.

Preheat the oven to 180°C (350°F), gas mark 4.

Heat a little oil in a large frying pan. Add the garlic and onion and cook until golden, then add the meat. Season with salt and pepper and add the wine. Simmer gently, uncovered, for 15 minutes. Snip the herbs with scissors and add to the frying pan with the chopped Swiss chard greens. Mix everything together well.

Heat a little oil in a pan and add the tomatoes and the celery. Season with salt and pepper. Simmer gently for 5 minutes until the mixture thickens slightly.

Lightly oil a baking dish. Arrange some of the lasagne sheets in the bottom of the dish, then spread with some of the tomato sauce followed by a layer of the meat mixture. Sprinkle with Parmesan and continue layering, finishing with a layer of Parmesan.

Bake in the preheated oven for 20-30 minutes.

Mexican lasagne

Serves 4-6

8 sheets precooked lasagne

1 green chilli

1 red chilli

2 onions, peeled

1 large red onion, peeled

3 garlic cloves, peeled

1 x 285 g (9 oz) can sweetcorn

1 ball mozzarella

2 x 400 g (14 oz) cans chopped tomatoes

2 chicken breast fillets, cut into small pieces

2 tablespoons olive oil

salt and freshly ground black pepper

Halve the chillies and remove the seeds. Blanch in boiling water for 5 minutes, then drain, pat dry with kitchen paper and cut into small pieces. Cut the 2 onions into eighths and thinly slice the red onion into rounds. Drain the sweetcorn. Drain the mozzarella and pat dry.

For the tomato sauce, put the tomatoes in the bowl of a food processor along with the garlic and the 2 onions. Process until finely chopped. Season with salt and pepper.

Preheat the oven to 180°C (350°F), gas mark 4.

Heat the oil in a frying pan over moderate heat, add the chicken breast pieces and chillies and cook for 10 minutes. When cooked, chop the chicken finely. Discard the chilli pieces if desired.

Lightly oil a baking dish and spoon in some of the tomato sauce, spreading it evenly over the base of the dish. Top with some lasagne sheets, chicken, chilli pieces (if retaining), tomato sauce, sweetcorn, and red onion. Continue layering until the dish is filled, finishing with a thin layer of sauce. Arrange the remaining red onion and slices of mozzarella on the top. Season with salt and pepper.

Bake in the preheated oven for about 40 minutes.

Fresh salmon lasagne

Serves 4-6

8 sheets precooked
lasagne

1 onion, peeled

1 carrot, peeled

1 bulb fennel, outer leaves
removed

1 lemon

1 bouquet garni

625 g (1¼ lb) salmon fillets

500 g (1 lb) fresh mussels

250 ml (9 fl oz) dry white
wine

2 egg yolks

1 bunch dill

1 bunch flat leaf parsley

olive oil

sea salt and freshly ground
black pepper

Thinly slice the onion, carrot and fennel bulb. Scrub the lemon and slice into thin rounds

To cook the salmon, prepare a court-bouillon by bringing 2 litres (3½ pints) water to the boil. Add the vegetables, lemon slices and bouquet garni. Season with sea salt and three turns of the peppermill and simmer gently for 7-8 minutes.

Wash the salmon fillets and pat dry. Place in the court-bouillon and poach for 10 minutes over gentle heat. Remove and drain well, then flake the flesh, discarding any skin and bones.

Preheat the oven to 180°C (350°F), gas mark 4.

Scrub and debeard the mussels, rinse well and put in a large pan. Add the wine and 2 turns of the peppermill. Cook over high heat, shaking occasionally until the mussels have opened, about 10 minutes. Remove from the heat and discard any that have not opened. Remove the mussels from their shells and strain the cooking liquor through a sieve lined with muslin.

In a bowl, whisk together the egg yolks and some of the mussel liquor, then top up with more liquor to obtain 500 ml (17 fl oz) of sauce. Add the mussels. Snip the herbs with scissors and add to the mussels.

Lightly oil a baking dish and arrange a few sheets of lasagne over the bottom. Cover with a layer of salmon and then a layer of sauce. Continue layering until all the ingredients are used, finishing with a layer of sauce.

Bake in the preheated oven for 20-30 minutes.

Cod and mangetout lasagne

Serves 4-6

8 sheets lasagne

1 fish stock cube

625 g (1¼ lb) cod fillets, fresh or frozen and defrosted

625 g (1¼ lb) mangetout

3 oranges

2 red onions

4 tablespoons olive oil

100g (3½ oz) pitted black olives

100 ml (3½ fl oz) soy sauce

200 ml (7 fl oz) oyster sauce

salt and freshly ground black pepper

Make a court-bouillon in a pan by dissolving the stock cube in a pint of water and bringing to the boil. Add the fish and return to a gentle simmer. As soon as the liquid begins to bubble, turn off the heat and let it stand while preparing and cooking the vegetables.

Wash and trim the mangetout. Grate the rind of 2 of the oranges and squeeze the juice. Peel and separate the third orange into segments, removing the membrane. Peel the onions and slice thinly.

Preheat the oven to 180°C (350°F), gas mark 4.

Heat the oil in a large frying pan. Add the mangetout, onion, orange zest, black olives and soy sauce. Stir well and cook for 5 minutes. Add the oyster sauce and taste for seasoning.

To cook the lasagne sheets, put the orange juice in a large pan, add water and bring to the boil. Cook the lasagne sheets for 2-3 minutes. Refresh under cold, running water. Pat dry on kitchen paper.

Drain the cod and flake the flesh, discarding the skin and bones.

Lightly oil a baking dish. Arrange some lasagne sheets over the bottom of the dish, then top with a layer of vegetables, orange segments and cod. Continue layering until all the ingredients are used.

Bake in the preheated oven for 20-25 minutes.

Sardine and grilled pepper lasagne

Serves 4-6

8 sheets precooked
lasagne

3 red peppers

1 green pepper

1 fish stock cube

180 g (5 oz) unsalted butter,
diced

olive oil

14 fresh sardine fillets

½ bunch coriander

herb salt and freshly ground
black pepper

Wash the peppers. Put 2 of the red peppers and the green pepper on a grill pan and cook under a hot grill under charred all over. Seal the peppers in a plastic bag and allow to stand for 15 minutes before peeling off the skin and removing the seeds. Slice the flesh thinly.

Deseed the remaining red pepper and cut into dice. In a pan, dissolve the stock cube in 200 ml (7 fl oz) water. Bring to a simmer, add the diced red pepper and cook for 7-8 minutes, then process to a purée in a food processor or blender.

Preheat the oven to 180°C (350°F), gas mark 4.

Warm the red pepper purée over low heat and add the butter piece by piece, whisking constantly. Taste for seasoning.

Lightly oil a baking dish. Spread a little of the pepper purée over the bottom of the dish. Top with a layer of lasagne sheets, then sardine fillets, coriander leaves, a sprinkling of herb salt and slices of grilled peppers. Repeat the layers until the ingredients are used up, finishing with the pepper purée.

Bake in the preheated oven for 25-35 minutes.

Smoked salmon lasagne

Serves 6 as a starter

6 sheets lasagne

350 g (10 oz) cottage cheese

200 ml (7 fl oz) crème fraîche

1 tablespoon coarse-grain mustard

1 bunch mixed fresh herbs (chives, parsley, etc.)

1–2 mini cucumbers

6 slices smoked salmon

½ bunch chervil

salt and freshly ground black pepper

Combine the cottage cheese, crème fraîche and mustard and whisk together thoroughly. Taste for seasoning. Snip the mixed herbs with scissors and add to the cottage cheese mixture, stirring to blend.

Wash the cucumber and slice into thin rounds.

Cook the lasagne sheets according to instructions on the packet. Drain and leave to dry on kitchen paper. Cut each sheet across in half.

On indiviual plates, arrange one half sheet of lasagne, one half slice of salmon, a spoonful of the cottage cheese mixture and a cucumber slice. Continue layering the salmon, cheese and cucumber, finishing with a half sheet of lasagne, decorated with chervil sprigs.

Curried crab lasagne

Serves 4-6

8 sheets of precooked lasagne

500 g (1 lb) cooked crab meat (or surimi, or a mix of shellfish and white fish fillets)

2 shallots

1 Granny Smith apple

50 g (2 oz) unsalted butter

1 tablespoon Madras curry powder

1 teaspoon turmeric

1 teaspoon coarsely crushed coriander seeds

grated rind and juice of 1 lime

500 ml (17 fl oz) Béchamel sauce (see recipe page 4)

salt

Preheat the oven to 180°C (350°F), gas mark 4.

Flake the crab meat. Peel the shallots and chop finely.

Leaving the apple unpeeled, cut it in half, remove the core, and slice thinly.

For the sauce, melt the butter in a large pan. Add the shallots and apple slices, and cook until translucent. Stir in the curry powder, turmeric, coriander seeds, lime zest and juice, and the crab meat. Add the Béchamel sauce and mix well. The sauce should not be too thick so dilute with a little milk if necessary. Taste for seasoning.

Lightly oil a baking dish. Arrange a layer of lasagne over the bottom of the dish, then add a layer of the crab mixture. Continue layering until all the ingredients are used up, finishing with a layer of lasagne.

Dot the surface with some butter and bake in the preheated oven for 25-30 minutes.

Spicy aubergine and prawn lasagne

Serves 4-6

8 sheets precooked lasagne

3 aubergines

3 garlic cloves, peeled

1 bunch spring onions

1 bunch flat leaf parsley

juice of 2 limes

200 ml (7 fl oz) olive oil

1/4 habanero chilli (Scotch Bonnet), finely chopped (discard the seeds if less 'heat' is required)

300 g (10 oz) fresh uncooked prawns

1 teaspoon paprika

juice of 1 lemon

1 x 400 g (14 oz) can chopped tomatoes

salt and freshly ground black pepper

3 sprigs fresh coriander (optional), to serve

Preheat oven to 190°C (375°F), gas mark 5.

Wash and dry the aubergines, cut in half lengthways and bake in the preheated oven for 30-40 minutes. Remove from the oven and reduce the heat to 180°C (350°F), gas mark 4.

Meanwhile, thinly slice the garlic and spring onions and place in a bowl. Wash the parsley, snip with scissors and add to the garlic mixture, along with the lime juice, oil, and finely chopped chilli. Season with salt and mix well. Stir in 175 ml (6 fl oz) hot water.

Peel the prawns and remove the intestinal black thread with the tip of a sharp knife. Add the prawns to the chilli mixture and allow to marinate for 30 minutes.

When the aubergines are cooked, scoop the flesh out into a bowl and crush with a fork. Add the paprika, lemon juice and tomatoes and mix together well. Season with salt and pepper. If the mixture is too thick, dilute with a few spoonfuls of the prawn marinade.

Lightly oil a baking dish. Place a layer of lasagne sheets in the bottom of the dish, top with some of the aubergine mixture, then add some coarsely chopped prawns and more aubergine. Continue layering until the dish is filled.

Bake in the preheated oven for 20-25 minutes. Decorate with fresh coriander leaves before serving, if desired.

Black lasagne

Serves 4-6

400 g (14 oz) plain flour, or, preferably, Italian pasta flour

4 eggs

2 packets of squid ink (about 4 g (1/8 oz) each)

1 kg (2 lb) prepared calamari

4 large tomatoes

1 garlic clove, peeled

3 tablespoons olive oil

1/2 bunch coriander

salt and freshly ground black pepper

Place the flour in a pile on a clean work surface and make a well in the middle. Break the eggs into the well and add the contents of 1 packet of squid ink. Wearing protective gloves to prevent staining from the squid ink, use your hands to combine the egg and flour mixture into a dough. (See instructions for homemade pasta on page 5.) Form into a ball and knead - the dough should be marbled. Continue kneading until the colour becomes uniform. Leave to stand at room temperature for 30 minutes.

Wash the calamari and cut into rings (if not already done). Plunge the tomatoes into boiling water for 1 minute, prick with the point of a sharp knife, then peel, deseed and chop the flesh coarsely. Finely chop the garlic.

Preheat the oven to 180°C (350°F), gas mark 4.

Heat the oil in a large pan. Add the calamari, tomatoes, garlic and the remaining packet of squid ink. Cook for 10 minutes, stirring constantly. Snip the coriander leaves with scissors and add to the pan. Season with salt and pepper, mixing well.

Place the dough on a floured surface and knead until smooth and supple. Roll out thinly with a rolling pin, or use a pasta machine. Cut into sheets to fit the baking dish.

Cook the pasta sheets in boiling, salted water for 3-4 minutes. Refresh under cold running water then dry on kitchen paper.

Lightly oil the baking dish. Place a layer of lasagne sheets in the bottom of the dish, then add a layer of the calamari mixture. Continue layering, finishing with a thin layer of the calamari mixture.

Bake in the preheated oven for 20-25 minutes.

Vegetarian lasagne

Serves 4-6

8–10 sheets lasagne verde

1 kg (2¼ lb) spinach

300 g (10 oz) ricotta

100 g (3½ oz) crème fraîche

nutmeg

1 bunch basil

1 x 400 g (14 oz) can
chopped tomatoes

50 g (2 oz) pine nuts

olive oil

salt and freshly ground
black pepper

Preheat the oven to 180ºC (350ºF), gas mark 4.

Wash and trim the spinach, then cook in a large pan of boiling salted water for 5 minutes. Transfer to a colander to drain, pushing down with a wooden spoon or squeezing by hand to extract all the water.

In a large bowl, combine the ricotta and crème fraiche. Season with salt, pepper and a pinch or two of freshly grated nutmeg.

Wash the basil, snip with scissors and combine with the tomatoes.

Cook the lasagne sheets in a large pan of boiling salted water according to the instructions on the packet. Refresh under cold running water. Leave to drain well on kitchen paper.

Lightly oil a baking dish. Spread a thin layer of ricotta mixture over the bottom, then top with some lasagne sheets. Spread a layer of coarsely chopped spinach on top, sprinkle with some pine nuts and some of the tomato. Continue layering, finishing with tomato and a sprinkling of pine nuts.

Bake in the preheated oven for 20-25 minutes.

All-tomato lasagne

Serves 4-6

8 sheets precooked lasagne

2 kg (4½ lb) ripe tomatoes

1 onion, peeled

2 garlic cloves, peeled

1 stick of celery

3 tablespoons olive oil

50 g (2 oz) pitted black olives

½ bunch basil

paprika

175 g (6oz) sun-dried tomatoes packed in oil

50 g (2 oz) freshly grated Parmesan cheese

salt and freshly ground black pepper

Plunge the tomatoes into boiling water for 1 minute, prick with the point of a sharp knife, then remove the skins. Deseed and chop the flesh coarsely. Finely chop the onion and garlic. Wash the celery and slice thinly.

Preheat the oven to 180ºC (350ºF), gas mark 4.

For the tomato sauce, heat the oil in a large pan. Add the onion and garlic and cook until soft. Add the fresh tomatoes, celery, olives and basil leaves. Season with salt, pepper and a pinch of paprika. Cook for 15 minutes, stirring occasionally. Transfer to a food processor and mix until puréed.

Lightly oil a baking dish. Spread a thin layer of tomato sauce over the bottom of the dish, then top with lasagne sheets and some sun-dried tomatoes. Continue layering, finishing with a layer of tomato sauce and a few sun-dried tomatoes. Sprinkle with the Parmesan cheese.

Bake in the preheated oven for 25-30 minutes.

Roasted vegetable lasagne

Serves 4-6

8 sheets lasagne

2 yellow peppers

2 red peppers

2 green peppers

4 courgettes

3 aubergines

1 red onion, peeled

1 bunch sage

8 tablespoons olive oil

juice of 1 lemon

1 garlic clove, peeled and crushed

250 ml (9 fl oz) lemon juice

salt and freshly ground black pepper

Wash the vegetables. Arrange all the peppers in a grill pan and cook under a hot grill until charred all over. Remove from the grill and place in a plastic bag. Seal tightly and leave to stand for 15 minutes. Remove the peppers, peel, deseed and cut the flesh into thin strips.

Cut the courgettes, aubergines and onion lengthways into thin strips. Brush with oil, sprinkle with chopped sage leaves, and place under a hot grill.

In a large bowl, combine 4 tablespoons of the oil, the lemon juice, garlic, salt and pepper. When the vegetables are cooked, add them to the mixture and coat well. Add the strips of pepper.

Preheat the oven to 180°C (350°F), gas mark 4.

Cook the lasagne in a large pan of boiling salted water with the 250 ml (9 fl oz) lemon juice according to the instructions on the packet. Rinse under cold running water, then drain on kitchen paper.

Lightly oil a baking dish. Arrange a layer of lasagne sheets over the bottom of the dish and brush lightly with olive oil. Top with a layer of vegetables and sprinkle with sage leaves. Continue layering until the dish is filled, finishing with a layer of vegetables.

Bake in the preheated oven for 20-25 minutes.

Summer vegetable lasagne

Serves 4-6

9 sheets lasagne, verde
or plain

1 bunch thin, tender carrots

500 g (1 lb) baby turnips
or large salad onions

2 shallots, peeled

1 garlic clove, peeled

100 g (3½ oz) rocket

1 bunch chervil

1 bunch basil

200 ml (7 fl oz) olive oil

100 ml (3½ fl oz) white wine
or sherry vinegar

2 teaspoons sugar

sea salt and freshly ground
black pepper

Peel or scrub the carrots and peel the turnips. Cut the carrots into rounds and halve the turnips widthways. Finely chop the shallots and garlic. Wash the rocket, chervil and basil and pat dry. Tear the rocket leaves into pieces, if large, and mix with most of the chervil leaves.

Preheat the oven to 180°C (350°F), gas mark 4.

Heat half of the oil in a pan. Add the turnips and cook until browned. Add half of the wine or sherry vinegar, 1 teaspoon of the sugar, a little salt and pepper and 250 ml (9 fl oz) water. Simmer gently until syrupy, 15-20 minutes.

Blanch the carrots in boiling salted water for 5 minutes, then drain. Heat the remaining olive oil in another pan. Add the shallots and garlic and cook until golden. Add the carrots, the remaining sugar and wine, and season with salt and pepper. Cook for 3 minutes. Remove from the heat and add some basil leaves that have been snipped with scissors.

Cook the lasagne in a large pan of boiling salted water according to the packet instructions. Drain, refresh under cold running water and cut each sheet in half to obtain 2 squares.

Lightly oil an ovenproof dish and arrange 6 lasagne squares in the bottom. Top each with some turnips and a few chervil leaves. Top with a lasagne square, then some carrots, then another lasagne square. Brush the top of each pasta square with oil.

Bake in the preheated oven for 5-8 minutes, just to warm the lasagne through.

Remove from the oven and transfer to plates with a wide spatula. Dress the mixed rocket and chervil leaves with some olive oil and a sprinkling of sea salt. Serve with the lasagne.

Artichoke lasagne

Serves 4-6

8–10 lasagne sheets

12 artichoke bottoms

juice of 1 lemon

3¹/₂ tablespoons olive oil

4 shallots, peeled

2 garlic cloves, peeled

6 slices of cheese suitable
for melting, such as mild
cheddar

2 teaspoons grated cheese,
such as Gruyère

salt and freshly ground
black pepper

If using frozen artichoke bottoms, cook according to packet instructions in boiling salted water with some lemon juice added. Canned artichoke bottoms should be rinsed well and tossed with lemon juice. Slice thinly.

Preheat the oven to 180°C (350°F), gas mark 4.

Bring a large pan of water to the boil. Add some salt and 2 tablespoons olive oil. Cook the lasagne sheets according to instructions on the packet. Refresh under cold running water and arrange in a single layer on kitchen paper to dry.

Finely chop the shallots and garlic. Heat a little oil in a pan, add the shallots and garlic and cook until golden. Add the artichokes and cook for 5-6 minutes more. Season with salt and pepper.

Lightly oil a baking dish. Arrange some lasagne sheets over the bottom of the dish, then spread with a layer of the artichoke mixture. Top with 2 slices of cheese. Continue layering, finishing with a layer of cheese slices.

Sprinkle with the grated cheese and bake in the preheated oven for 20-30 minutes.

Wild mushroom lasagne

Serves 4-6

8 sheets precooked lasagne

100 g (3½ oz) dried wild mushrooms, such as porcini (cèpes)

2 shallots, peeled

2 tablespoons olive oil

1 bunch flat leaf parsley

200 g (7 oz) crème fraîche

150 g (5 oz) unsalted butter

1 heaped tablespoon plain flour

500 ml (17 fl oz) milk

nutmeg

100 g (3½ oz) freshly grated Parmesan cheese

salt and freshly grated black pepper

Soak the mushrooms in warm water until soft, then squeeze out the excess moisture with your hands.

Preheat the oven to 180°C (350°F), gas mark 4.

Chop the shallots. Heat the oil in a pan, add the shallots and cook until golden. Wash and snip the parsley with scissors. Add the mushrooms and parsley to the shallots. Stir in the crème fraîche and season with salt and pepper. Cook gently for 7-8 minutes.

Using 3 oz of the butter, the flour, milk and nutmeg, make a Béchamel sauce as described in the recipe on page 4. Cook slowly for about 10 minutes, stirring constantly.

Lightly oil a baking dish. Spread a thin layer of Béchamel sauce in the bottom of the dish, top with some lasagne sheets, more Béchamel, some mushrooms and dot with butter. Continue layering in this way until the ingredients are used up. Finish with a layer of Béchamel, sprinkled with the Parmesan and dotted with butter.

Bake in the preheated oven for 25-35 minutes.

Pumpkin and coriander lasagne

Serves 4-6

8 sheets lasagne

1 onion, peeled

750 g (1½ lb) pumpkin flesh

50 g (2 oz) butter

300 ml (½ pint) milk

2 tablespoons olive oil

4 egg yolks

ground cumin

1 bunch coriander

salt and freshly ground
black pepper

Preheat the oven to 180°C (350°F), gas mark 4.

Finely chop the onion and cut the pumpkin flesh into pieces. Melt the butter in a pan, add the onion and cook until golden. Add the pumpkin pieces and stir with a wooden spoon until coated evenly with the butter. Add the milk and season with salt and pepper. Cook for 15 minutes.

Bring a large pan of water to the boil. Add salt and some olive oil and cook the lasagne according to instructions on the packet. Rinse under cold running water then allow to dry on kitchen paper.

With a fork, crush the pumpkin pieces to obtain a coarse purée. Stir in the egg yolks and a pinch or two of cumin. Season to taste.

Lightly oil a baking dish. Arrange a layer of lasagne in the bottom of a dish and top with some of the pumpkin mixture and a sprinkling of coriander leaves. Continue layering in this way until the ingredients are used up, finishing with a layer of the pumpkin mixture.

Bake in the preheated oven for 20-30 minutes.

Lamb lasagne with prunes

Serves 4-6

8 sheets precooked
lasagne

1 onion, peeled

1 green pepper

250 g (8 oz) pitted prunes

500 ml (17 fl oz) meat stock,
warmed

2 tablespoons olive oil

500 g (1 lb) minced lamb

1 heaped tablespoon
cornflour

nutmeg

ground cumin

salt and freshly ground
black pepper

Peel the onion and chop finely. Halve the pepper, remove the seeds and cut the flesh into fine dice.

Soak the prunes in the warm stock for 10 minutes.

Preheat the oven to 180°C (350°F), gas mark 4.

Heat the oil in a large pan. Add the onion and cook until golden. Add the lamb and the diced pepper. When the meat has browned, sprinkle with the cornflour. Add the prunes and the meat stock and mix well. Stir in a pinch or two of freshly grated nutmeg and ground cumin and season to taste with salt and pepper. Cook until thick, about 10 minutes.

Lightly oil a baking dish. Spread with a layer of the lamb mixture and top with lasagne sheets. Continue layering until the dish is filled, finishing with a layer of lamb.

Bake in the preheated oven for 20-30 minutes.

Chicken, apricot and almond lasagne

Serves 4-6

8 sheets precooked lasagne

1 onion, peeled

250 g (8 oz) dried apricots

4 chicken breast fillets

50 g (2 oz) butter

500 ml (17 fl oz) chicken stock

2 tablespoons honey

$1/2$ teaspoon ground cumin

$1/2$ teaspoon ground cinnamon

50 g (2 oz) flaked almonds

salt and freshly ground black pepper

Finely chop the onion. Cut the apricots into pieces. Thinly slice the chicken.

Preheat the oven to 180°C (350°F), gas mark 4.

Melt the butter in a pan. Add the onion and chicken and cook until golden.

Warm the stock and stir in the honey. Pour into the chicken, add the apricots, cumin, cinnamon and some of the almonds. Season to taste with salt and pepper. Mix well and simmer for 15 minutes.

Lightly oil a baking dish. Spread a thin layer of the chicken mixture in the bottom of the dish then top with some lasagne. Continue layering until the dish is filled.

Sprinkle with the remaining almonds and bake in the preheated oven for 20-30 minutes.

Chocolate lasagne

Serves 4-6

300 g (10 oz) plain flour, or, preferably, Italian pasta flour

100 g (3½ oz) + 3 tablespoons cocoa

2 tablespoons icing sugar

6 eggs

500 ml (17 fl oz) milk

2 tablespoons caster sugar

300 g (10 oz) best quality (70% solids) dark chocolate, broken into pieces

butter

In a bowl, combine the flour, 100 g (3½ oz) of the cocoa and the icing sugar. Pile in a heap a clean work surface and make a well in the centre. Add 3 of the eggs and mix gently. If the ingredients are not blending well, add a few drops of water. (See recipe for homemade pasta on page 5.) Knead until you obtain a smooth and even-coloured dough (Alternatively, prepare in a food processor). Leave to stand at room temperature for 1 hour.

Preheat the oven to 180°C (350°F), gas mark 4.

Warm the milk in a pan and whisk in the remaining cocoa. In a heatproof bowl beat the 3 remaining eggs with the caster sugar. Gradually pour the hot milk onto the eggs, whisking constantly. Return to the pan and stir over low heat until the custard thickens and coats the back of a spoon.

Lightly flour a work surface and roll out the dough thinly using a rolling pin, or use a pasta machine. Cut the sheet of dough into pieces to fit in the baking dish. Cook the sheets in boiling water for 2 minutes. Refresh under cold running water and dry on kitchen paper.

Lightly butter the baking dish. Place a sheet of lasagne in the bottom of the dish and top with some of the chocolate pieces. Continue alternating layers of lasagne and chocolate, (reserving a few pieces of chocolate to decorate), finishing with a layer of chocolate. Pour in the custard.

Bake in the centre of the preheated oven for 35-45 minutes.

Remove from the oven and top immediately with the reserved pieces of chocolate that will melt from the heat. Serve warm.

Shopping

JEANNINE CROS
vintage linens, pages 17, 25, 31.

MUJI
dishtowel, page 33;
fork, page 41.

RENUE-MÉNAGE
dishes, pages 7, 31, 35, 47;
spatula, page 23.

RÉSONANCES
glasses, page 9.

LA SAMARITAINE
Riess gratin dishes, pages 13, 53, 61;
Le Creuset baking dish, pages 25, 27;
Guy Degrenne plate, page 19;
Staub dish, page 23;
Revol dish, pages 29, 49;
fork, page 17.

HABITAT
plate, page 17;
dish, page 21.

THE CONRAN SHOP
apron, page 57.

IKEA
plate, pages 51, 59;
saucer, page 55.

MONOPRIX
rectangular dish, pages 41, 63;
oval dishes, pages 43, 57;
plate, page, 11;
placemat, page 9.

Addresses

JEANNINE CROS
11 Rue d'Assas, 75006 Paris, France
tél. 01 45 48 00 67

MUJI
135 Long Acre, Covent Garden WC2E 9AD
tel. 020 7379 0820
www.muji.co.uk

RENUE-MÉNAGE
50 Rue des Abbesses, 75018 Paris, France
tél. 01 46 06 23 79

RÉSONANCES
9 Cour Saint-Émilion, 75012 Paris, France
tél. 01 44 73 82 82
www.resonances.fr

LA SAMARITAINE
19 Rue Monnaie, 75001 Paris, France
tél. 01 40 41 20 20
www.lasamaritaine.com

HABITAT
196 Tottenham Court Road, WIT 7LG
tel. 020 7631 3880
www.habitat.net

THE CONRAN SHOP
Michelin House, 81 Fulham Road SW3 6RD
tel. 020 7589 7401
www.conran.com

IKEA
www.ikea.com

MONOPRIX
www.monoprix.fr

© Marabout 2004
This edition © Hachette Livre (Hachette Pratique) 2005
This edition published by Hachette Illustrated UK, Octopus Publishing Group,
2–4 Heron Quays, London E14 4JP

English translation by JMS Books LLP (email: moseleystrachan@dsl.pipex.com)
Translation © Octopus Publishing Group

A CIP catalogue for this book is available from the British Library

ISBN 10: 1 84430 134 6

ISBN 13: 978 1 84430 134 8

Printed by Toppan Printing Co., (HK) Ltd.